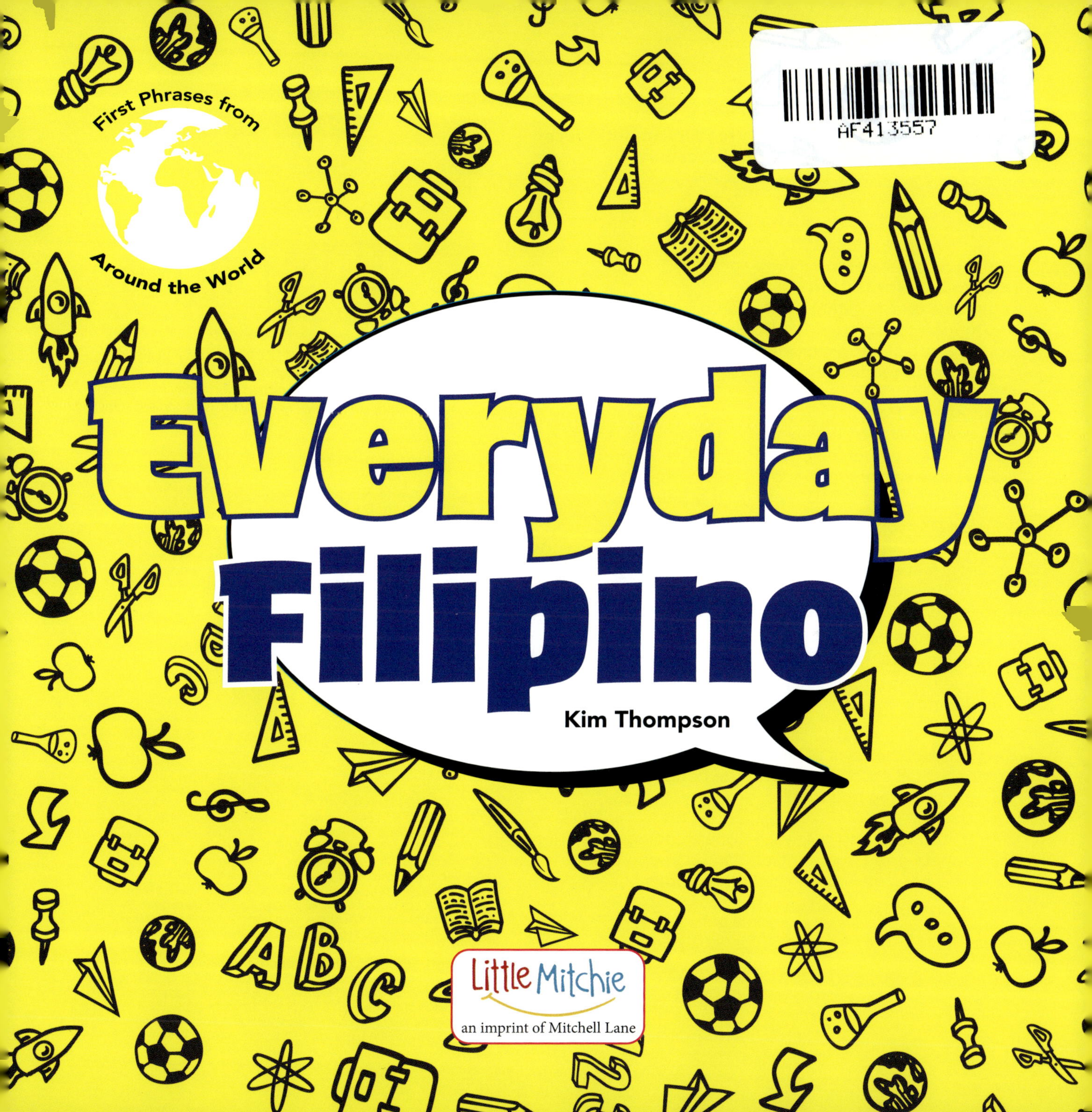

First Phrases from Around the World
Everyday Filipino
Kim Thompson
Little Mitchie
an imprint of Mitchell Lane

Creating Young Nonfiction Readers

Little Mitchie lets children delve into nonfiction at beginning reading levels. Young readers are introduced to new concepts, facts, ideas, and vocabulary.

Tips for Reading Nonfiction with Young Readers

Talk about Nonfiction
Begin by explaining that nonfiction books give us information that is true. The book will be organized around a specific topic or idea, and we may learn new facts through reading.

Look at the Parts
Most nonfiction books have helpful features. Our *Little Mitchie* titles include color photographs and graphic aids, a table of contents, and an index. Share the purpose of these features with your reader.

Color Photos and Graphic Aids
A lot of information can be found by "reading" photos, charts, maps, and other graphic aids found within nonfiction texts. Help your reader learn more about the different ways information can be displayed.

Table of Contents
Located at the front of the book, this list shows the big ideas within the text and the page numbers where they can be found.

Index
Located at the back of the book, an index is an alphabetical list of topics and the page numbers where they can be found.

With a little help and guidance about reading nonfiction, you can feel good about introducing a young reader to the world of *Little Mitchie* nonfiction books.

Mitchell Lane
PUBLISHERS

2001 SW 31st Avenue
Hallandale, FL 33009
www.mitchelllanepub.com

Little Mitchie

First Edition, 2026.

Author: Kim Thompson
Designer: Kathy Walsh
Editor: Tricia Hoffman

Names/credits: Kim Thompson
Title: First Phrases from Around the World
 Everyday Filipino
Description: Hallandale, FL:
Mitchell Lane Publishers, [2026]

Series: First Phrases from Around the World
Library bound ISBN: 979-8-89260-539-7
Paperback ISBN: 979-8-89260-581-6
eBook ISBN: 979-8-89260-550-2

Little Mitchie is an imprint of
Mitchell Lane Publishers

PHOTO CREDITS
Cover and Title pg: Adobe Stock: iukhym_vova, smile3377; Doodle Art Adobe: devitaayu, FourLeafLover, wanchana, veekicl, Rizky, mhatzapa, Kebon doodle, Asyam Design, piixypeach, syoko: istock: background, rica nohara; p4, 6 3bugsmom; p5, FatCamera, rizal999; p6, monkeybusinessimages, p7, StefaNikolic, SolStock; p 9, 3sbworld; p 13, Bet_Noire; p 16, dimarik, FatCamera, kate_sept2004; p 18, FatCamera, Satoshi-K, manley 099; p 19 SDI Productions, kate_sept2004; p 22, Petri Oeschger, EyeEm Mobile GmbH, Kdshutterman, FatCamera; Shutterstock: p4, TimeImage Production; p6Anatoliy Karlyuk; p7, Eric Isselee; p 10, Q88; p 11, Svetlyachock, p 12, PeopleImages.com - Yuri A, Chiociolla, BongoStock, Zaleman; p 13 Q88; p 14, wavebreakmedia, Q88, 88STOCKVN, p 15, Studio Romantic, Monkey Business Images; p 17, ziggy_mars; p 20, ESB Professional, 88STOCKVN, StockImageFactory.com, Max kegfire; p 21, Kravtzov, Louis Go, Lisyl, tomas del amo, sri widyowati, Ivan Trizlic

Table of Contents

This Is Me

Ang pangalan ko ay Carmelita.

My name is Carmelita.

Ito Ako

isa
one
dalawa
two
tatlo
three
apat
four
lima
five
anim
six
pito
seven
walo
eight
siyam
nine
sampu
ten
Paalam!
Goodbye!

People and Pets

6

Mga Tao at Mga Alagang Hayop

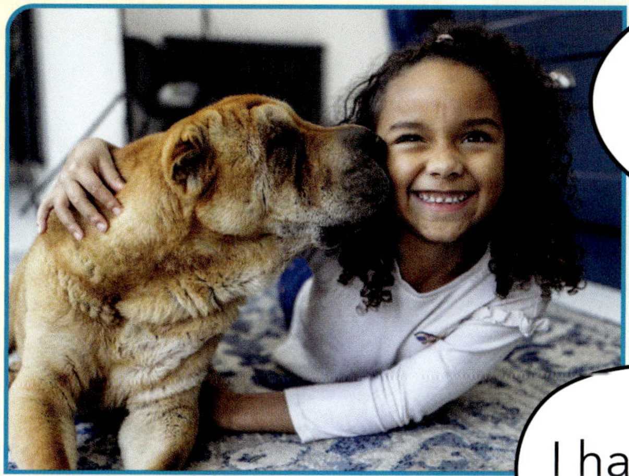

Mayroon akong mga alagang hayop.

I have pets.

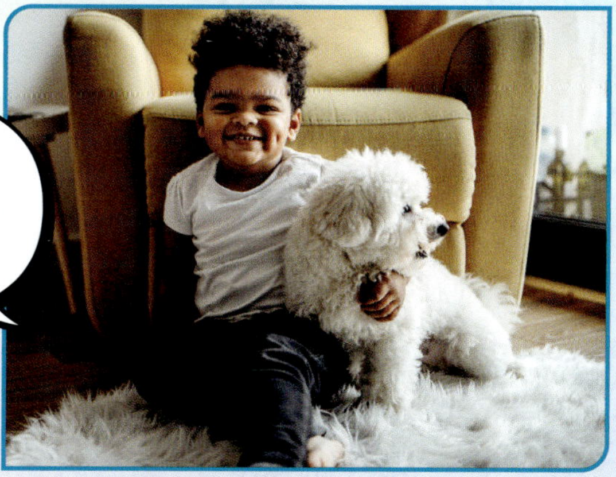

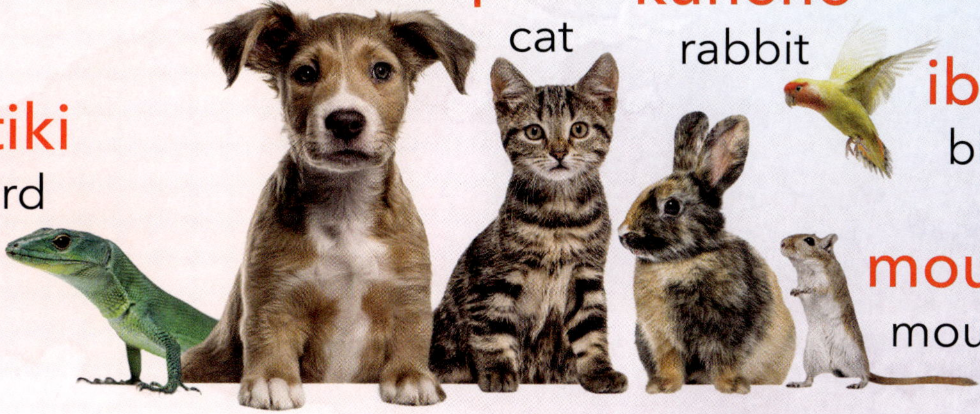
aso
dog
pusa
cat
kuneho
rabbit
ibon
bird
butiki
lizard
mouse
mouse

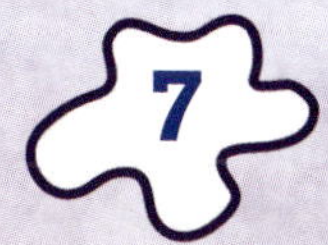

Today

Ngayon ay Biyernes.
Today is Friday.

Linggo
Sunday

Lunes
Monday

Martes
Tuesday

Miyerkules
Wednesday

Huwebes
Thursday

Biyernes
Friday

Sabado
Saturday

Ang buwan ay Marso.
The month is March.

Enero	January
Pebrero	February
Marso	March
Abril	April
Mayo	May
Hunyo	June
Hulyo	July
Agosto	August
Setyembre	September
Oktubre	October
Nobyembre	November
Disyembre	December

Ngayong araw

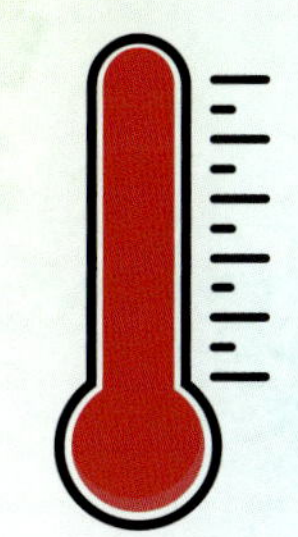

Morning

Sinusuklay ko ang buhok ko.

I comb my hair.

Nagtoothbrush ako.

I brush my teeth.

Umaga

Naka-pink na medyas ako.

I wear pink socks.

kahel
orange

dilaw
yellow

asul
blue

berde
green

pula
red

rosas
pink

lila
purple

itim
black

puti
white

Breakfast

tinapay
bread

katas ng dalandan
orange juice

gatas
milk

itlog
egg

bus ng paaralan
school bus

salamin sa mata
eyeglasses

School

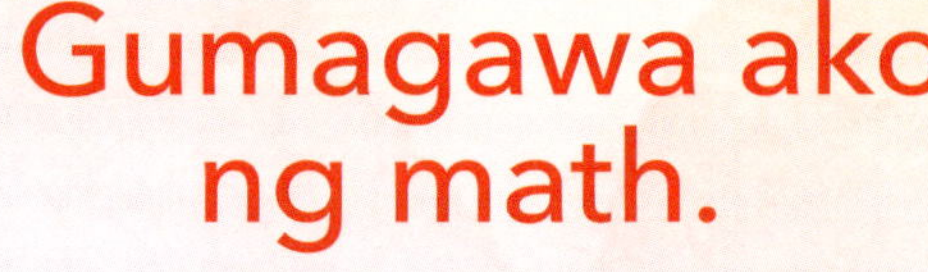

Nabasa ko.

I read.

Gumagawa ako ng math.

I do math.

Paaralan

desk
desk

guro
teacher

Time to Play

Paglalaruan mo ba ako?
Will you play with me?
Oo!
Yes!
Tumatakbo ako.
I run.
Nag-swing ako.
I swing.

Oras para Maglaro

17

Neighborhood

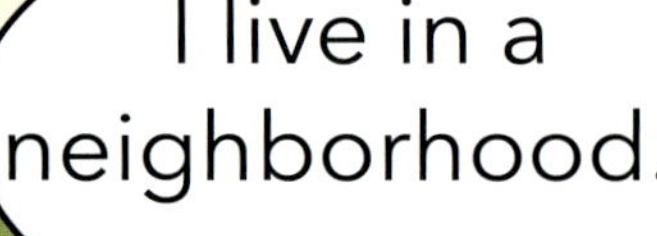

Kumaway ako sa kaibigan ko.
I wave to my friend.

Pumunta ako sa tindahan.
I go to the store.

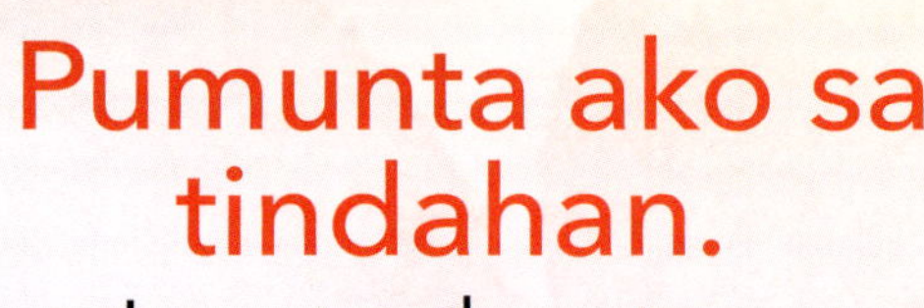

Kapitbahayan

puno
tree

bahay
house

bangketa
sidewalk

daan
road

bisikleta
bicycle

Dinner

Oo, pakiusap.
Yes, please.

Hindi, salamat.
No, thank you.

Ipagpaumanhin mo.
Excuse me.

Hapunan

adobo
stew

lechon
pork

halo-halo
frozen dessert

puto
rice cakes

inihaw na steak
grilled steak

Night

Naka-pajama ako.

I wear pajamas.

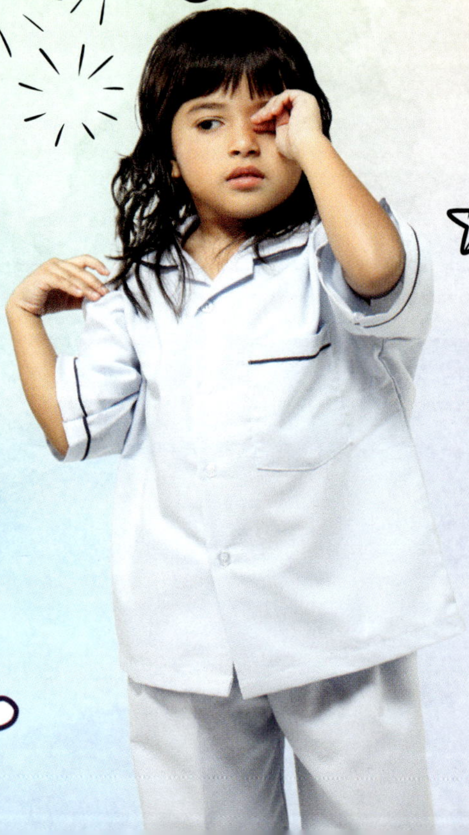

Humiga na ako.

I go to bed.

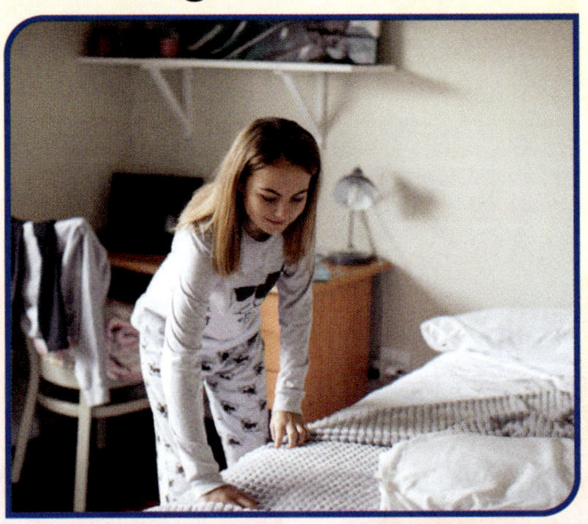

Pumikit ako.

I close my eyes.

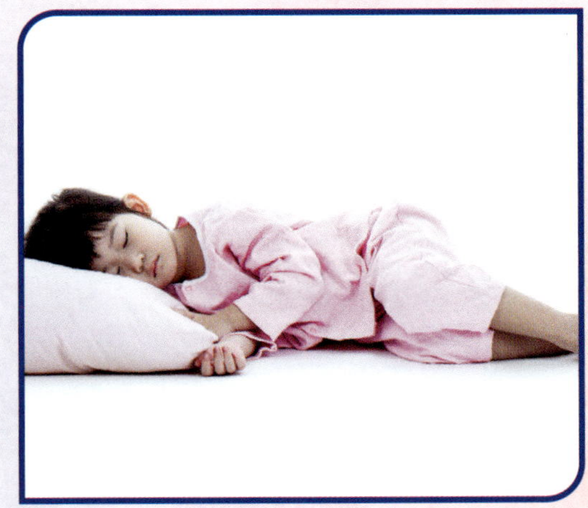

Gabi

Magandang gabi!

Good night!

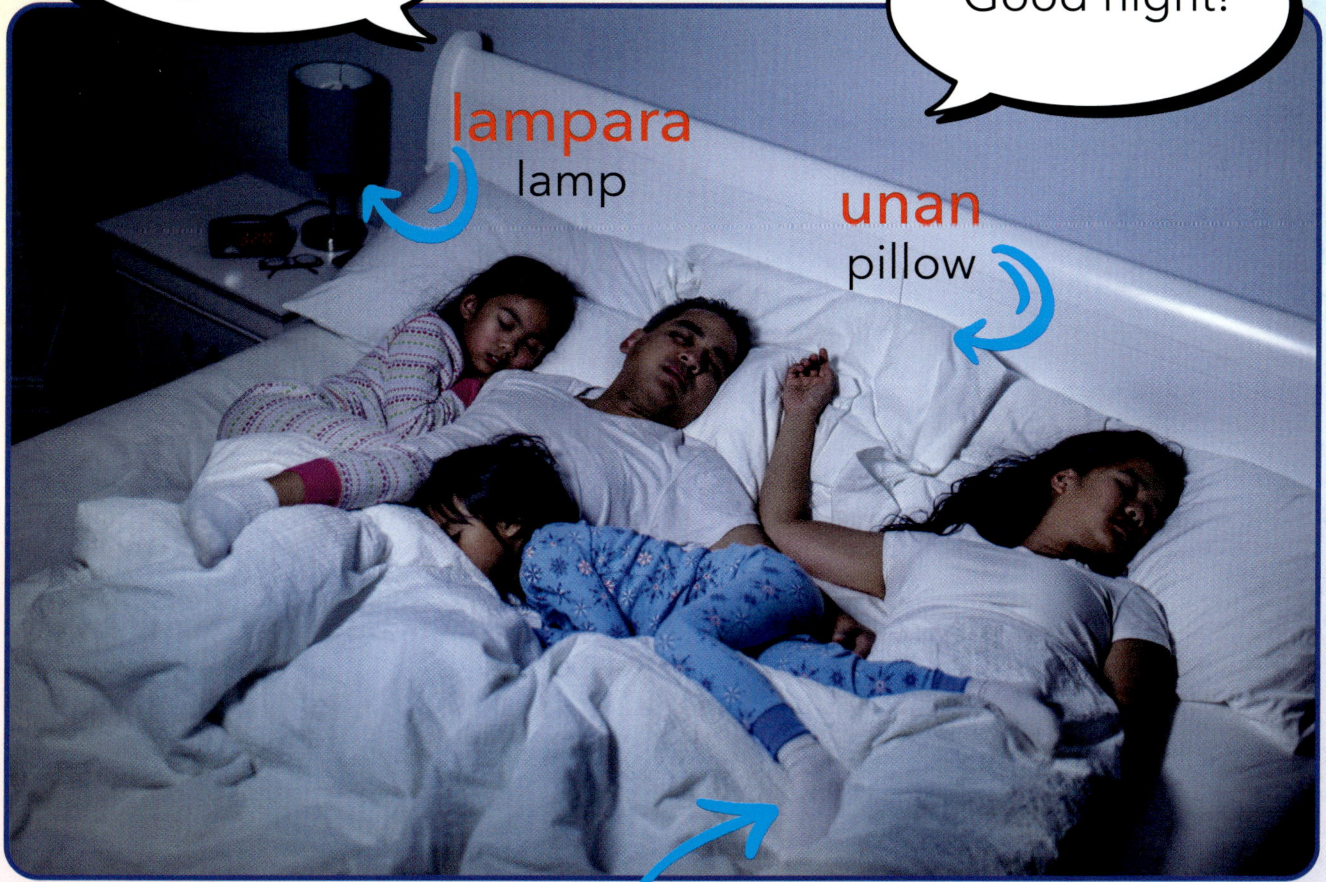

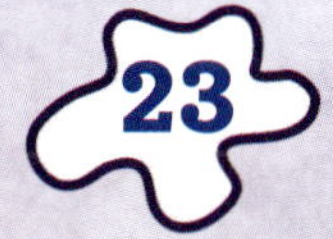

Index

About Filipino

Filipino is the official language of the Republic of the Philippines, a country in Southeast Asia. It is spoken by more than 90 million people in the Philippines. It is also spoken by nearly 10 million people in Filipino communities around the world. The language includes many words borrowed from English and Spanish. Children who speak Filipino learn to read quickly because each letter of the alphabet makes just one sound. A polite form of Filipino is used when addressing strangers or people who are older than you.